Copyright © 2023 by S. J. Matthews (Author)

This book is protected by copyright law and is intended solely for personal use. Reproduction, distribution, or any other form of use requires the written permission of the author. The information presented in this book is for educational and entertainment purposes only, and while every effort has been made to ensure its accuracy and completeness, no guarantees are made. The author is not providing legal, financial, medical, or professional advice, and readers should consult with a licensed professional before implementing any of the techniques discussed in this book. The content in this book has been sourced from various reliable sources, but readers should exercise their own judgment when using this information. The author is not responsible for any losses, direct or indirect, that may occur from the use of this book, including but not limited to errors, omissions, or inaccuracies.

We hope this book has been informative and helpful on your journey to understanding and celebrating older adults. Thank you for your interest and support!

Title: The Future of Digital Gold
Subtitle: Navigating the Opportunities and Challenges of Bitcoin

Series: Decoding Satoshi's White Paper: A Three-Part Exploration of Bitcoin's Origins and Impact

By S. J. Matthews

"Bitcoin is a remarkable cryptographic achievement and the ability to create something that is not duplicable in the digital world has enormous value."
Eric Schmidt, former CEO of Google

"Bitcoin is the beginning of something great: a currency without a government, something necessary and imperative."
Nassim Taleb, author and economist

"The Bitcoin white paper is one of the most important innovations of our time, and it has the potential to change the way we think about money and finance forever."
Marc Andreessen, co-founder of Netscape and venture capitalist

"Satoshi's white paper on Bitcoin represents one of the most profound technological breakthroughs of our time. It's a blueprint for a new financial system that can be trusted, secure, and accessible to all."
Wences Casares, CEO of Xapo

"The Bitcoin white paper is a revolutionary piece of technology that has the potential to disrupt traditional financial systems and change the way we interact with money."

Andreas Antonopoulos, author and Bitcoin educator

Table of Contents

Introduction 7
Discussion of the wider implications of Bitcoin beyond finance 7
Overview of the social, political, and economic implications of Bitcoin 10
Introduction to the potential future of Bitcoin and its impact on society 14

Chapter 1: Bitcoin and the Future of Finance 17
The potential impact of Bitcoin on the traditional financial system 17
The potential for Bitcoin to be used as a store of value 20
The role of decentralized finance (DeFi) in the future of Bitcoin and financial transactions 22

Chapter 2: Bitcoin and Privacy 25
The importance of privacy in digital transactions 25
The potential for Bitcoin to enhance privacy in financial transactions 28
The challenges and limitations of privacy in the Bitcoin system 30

Chapter 3: Bitcoin and Globalization 32
The potential impact of Bitcoin on international trade and commerce 32
The role of Bitcoin in enabling cross-border transactions . 35
The potential for Bitcoin to reduce transaction costs and improve financial inclusion 37

Chapter 4: Bitcoin and Society 40
The potential social implications of Bitcoin 40
The impact of Bitcoin on income inequality and wealth distribution 46
The role of Bitcoin in enabling new forms of economic organization and social change 49
Chapter 5: Bitcoin and Regulation 52
The current regulatory landscape for Bitcoin and digital currencies 52
The challenges and opportunities of regulating Bitcoin 55
The potential for government intervention in the Bitcoin system 58
Conclusion 61
The broader implications of Bitcoin beyond finance, including privacy, globalization, and societal impact 61
The potential for further development and innovation in the Bitcoin system 64
The importance of continued research and discussion around the future of Bitcoin and its impact on society 66
Key Terms and Definitions 68
Supporting Materials 70
Bitcoin Whitepaper 70
Potential References 72

Introduction
Discussion of the wider implications of Bitcoin beyond finance

Bitcoin was first introduced in 2008 as a decentralized digital currency that would allow for peer-to-peer transactions without the need for intermediaries such as banks. While Bitcoin has certainly made waves in the financial industry, its implications go far beyond finance. In this section, we will discuss the wider implications of Bitcoin beyond finance.

One of the most significant implications of Bitcoin is its potential to disrupt the traditional financial system. The use of blockchain technology enables Bitcoin to offer a secure and transparent alternative to the traditional banking system, which is often characterized by high fees, slow transaction times, and a lack of transparency. By allowing individuals to transact directly with each other, Bitcoin has the potential to reduce the need for traditional financial institutions, particularly in developing countries where access to banking services is limited.

Another implication of Bitcoin is its potential to promote financial inclusion. By enabling peer-to-peer transactions, Bitcoin has the potential to provide financial services to individuals who are unbanked or underbanked.

This could have a significant impact on poverty reduction and economic development in developing countries.

Bitcoin also has the potential to enhance privacy in digital transactions. The use of cryptography in Bitcoin transactions means that users can transact without revealing their identity, which can be particularly important in countries where freedom of speech is limited, and government surveillance is prevalent.

In addition to the financial implications, Bitcoin has significant social, political, and economic implications. For example, Bitcoin has the potential to enable new forms of economic organization, such as decentralized autonomous organizations (DAOs). DAOs are organizations that operate on blockchain technology and are governed by smart contracts. They have the potential to disrupt traditional forms of economic organization and could have significant implications for the future of work.

Bitcoin could also have significant implications for international trade and commerce. The use of Bitcoin could enable cross-border transactions to occur more quickly and with lower transaction costs. This could have a significant impact on international trade and could promote economic growth in developing countries.

Finally, Bitcoin's implications go beyond economics and could have significant social and political implications. The use of Bitcoin could promote greater individual sovereignty and could challenge traditional power structures. This could have significant implications for the future of democracy and the role of government in society.

In conclusion, Bitcoin's implications go far beyond finance. It has the potential to disrupt traditional power structures, promote financial inclusion, enhance privacy in digital transactions, and enable new forms of economic organization. As we move forward, it will be important to continue to explore these implications and to consider how Bitcoin can be used to promote a more just and equitable society.

Overview of the social, political, and economic implications of Bitcoin

Bitcoin, as a decentralized digital currency, has far-reaching social, political, and economic implications beyond the financial sector. This chapter provides an overview of these implications and explores how they are shaping the future of society.

Social Implications

Bitcoin is a revolutionary technology that can transform the way we interact with each other. It has the potential to create a more transparent and equitable society by democratizing access to financial services. Bitcoin can also facilitate the creation of new forms of social organization that are independent of traditional institutions. For example, it can enable decentralized autonomous organizations (DAOs), which are run by code and not controlled by any single individual or entity. These DAOs can facilitate the creation of decentralized communities that can work together towards a common goal.

Another important social implication of Bitcoin is its potential to improve financial inclusion. Bitcoin can enable people who lack access to traditional financial services to participate in the global economy. This can help reduce poverty and promote economic development in underserved communities. Moreover, Bitcoin can help protect the financial rights of individuals by providing them with a means to store and transfer value without the need for intermediaries.

However, there are also social challenges associated with Bitcoin. The decentralized and anonymous nature of Bitcoin can make it difficult to trace criminal activity. Bitcoin has been associated with illegal activities such as money laundering, tax evasion, and drug trafficking. Moreover, the use of Bitcoin can perpetuate existing social inequalities, as individuals with greater access to technology and financial resources are more likely to benefit from the use of Bitcoin.

Political Implications

Bitcoin has significant political implications as it challenges the traditional role of governments in regulating financial systems. Bitcoin operates outside of government control, and as such, it can be used to circumvent capital controls and economic sanctions. This can create challenges for governments in maintaining financial stability and enforcing monetary policy.

Moreover, the decentralized and transparent nature of Bitcoin can empower individuals and communities by giving them greater control over their financial assets. This can reduce dependence on centralized financial institutions and potentially limit the influence of governments over financial systems. However, this can also create challenges for governments in ensuring the stability and security of the financial system.

Another political implication of Bitcoin is its potential to promote individual freedom and autonomy. Bitcoin enables individuals to store and transfer value without the need for intermediaries, which can help protect their financial privacy and rights. This can be particularly important in countries with weak rule of law and authoritarian regimes.

Economic Implications

Bitcoin has significant economic implications as it challenges the traditional role of financial institutions in managing the global economy. Bitcoin operates outside of traditional financial systems and as such, it can potentially disrupt existing economic structures. Bitcoin can facilitate cross-border transactions, reduce transaction costs, and promote financial inclusion.

Moreover, Bitcoin can serve as a store of value and a hedge against inflation. As a deflationary currency with a fixed supply, Bitcoin can potentially increase in value over time. This can provide individuals with a means to protect their wealth from inflation and currency devaluation.

However, Bitcoin also has economic challenges. The volatility of Bitcoin prices can create uncertainty and limit its usefulness as a medium of exchange. Moreover, the decentralized nature of Bitcoin can make it difficult to regulate and enforce consumer protection laws, which can create risks for investors and consumers.

In conclusion, Bitcoin has significant social, political, and economic implications beyond the financial sector. While it has the potential to create a more transparent, equitable, and inclusive society, it also presents significant challenges. It is important for policymakers, regulators, and society as a whole to continue to explore and understand these implications as Bitcoin continues to evolve and shape the future of society.

Introduction to the potential future of Bitcoin and its impact on society

Bitcoin is more than just a decentralized digital currency. It has the potential to fundamentally change the way society operates and interacts with money. In this section, we will explore the potential future of Bitcoin and its impact on society.

First, it is important to understand that Bitcoin's potential future is highly uncertain. While it has gained significant momentum over the past decade, it still faces many challenges and obstacles. Nonetheless, the potential future of Bitcoin is exciting and worth exploring.

One potential future of Bitcoin is that it becomes a widely accepted and used currency, similar to the US dollar or the euro. If this were to happen, it could significantly disrupt the traditional financial system and change the way people interact with money. Transactions could become faster and cheaper, and financial services could become more widely available to people around the world.

Another potential future of Bitcoin is that it becomes a store of value, similar to gold. In this scenario, people may use Bitcoin as a hedge against inflation or economic instability, similar to how people have traditionally used gold. This could lead to a significant increase in the value of

Bitcoin over time, and it could become a mainstream asset class.

Bitcoin could also play a significant role in improving financial inclusion, especially in countries with underdeveloped financial systems. Bitcoin's decentralized nature makes it accessible to anyone with an internet connection, which means that people who are excluded from traditional financial systems could potentially gain access to financial services through Bitcoin.

However, Bitcoin's potential future is not without challenges. One of the biggest challenges is the regulatory landscape. Governments around the world are still grappling with how to regulate Bitcoin and other cryptocurrencies, and there is a risk that overly restrictive regulations could stifle innovation and growth in the industry.

Another challenge is scalability. As we discussed earlier, Bitcoin's current transaction processing capacity is limited, which could limit its potential future as a widely used currency. However, developments like the Lightning Network could potentially address this issue and enable faster and more efficient transactions.

In conclusion, Bitcoin's potential future is uncertain, but it is also exciting. It has the potential to fundamentally change the way society interacts with money and improve financial inclusion around the world. However, there are also challenges and obstacles that must be overcome. It will be important to continue researching and discussing the potential future of Bitcoin and its impact on society.

Chapter 1: Bitcoin and the Future of Finance

The potential impact of Bitcoin on the traditional financial system

Bitcoin has the potential to disrupt the traditional financial system in many ways. One of the most significant impacts of Bitcoin on the financial system is the decentralization of the system. Bitcoin allows for peer-to-peer transactions without the need for intermediaries such as banks or other financial institutions. This can potentially reduce transaction costs and increase transaction speed.

Another potential impact of Bitcoin on the financial system is the creation of new financial instruments. For example, Bitcoin can be used to create smart contracts that can execute automatically based on pre-programmed conditions. This can potentially eliminate the need for intermediaries such as lawyers and other legal professionals in financial transactions.

Bitcoin also has the potential to create new investment opportunities. For example, Bitcoin can be used as a store of value similar to gold or other commodities. In addition, the decentralized nature of Bitcoin allows for the creation of new investment vehicles such as Bitcoin exchange-traded funds (ETFs) that can be traded on traditional exchanges.

Bitcoin can also potentially increase financial inclusion by providing access to financial services for people who do not have access to traditional banking services. This is because Bitcoin can be used without the need for a bank account or other financial intermediaries. This can potentially help people in developing countries where access to banking services is limited.

However, there are also potential challenges and drawbacks of Bitcoin on the traditional financial system. One of the main challenges is the lack of regulation and oversight in the Bitcoin system. This can potentially lead to fraud, market manipulation, and other illicit activities.

Another challenge is the potential for Bitcoin to be used in illegal activities such as money laundering and terrorism financing. This can potentially lead to increased scrutiny from law enforcement and regulatory agencies.

In addition, the volatility of Bitcoin prices can make it difficult for traditional financial institutions to integrate Bitcoin into their operations. This is because Bitcoin prices can fluctuate rapidly and unpredictably, which can create significant risks for financial institutions.

Despite these challenges, the potential impact of Bitcoin on the traditional financial system is significant. Bitcoin has the potential to disrupt the traditional financial system in many ways and create new opportunities for investors and financial institutions alike. However, it is important to carefully consider the potential risks and drawbacks before investing in or adopting Bitcoin as a financial instrument.

The potential for Bitcoin to be used as a store of value

Bitcoin has been referred to as "digital gold" due to its similarities with the precious metal as a store of value. Gold has traditionally been used as a store of value due to its scarcity, durability, and relatively stable value over time. Bitcoin shares many of these characteristics, with its limited supply and decentralized nature making it a potentially valuable store of value.

One of the key features of Bitcoin as a store of value is its scarcity. Unlike fiat currencies, which can be printed or created by central banks at will, there is a limited supply of Bitcoin. The total number of Bitcoins that can ever exist is 21 million, and this limit is enforced by the code that underpins the Bitcoin network. This scarcity is similar to gold, which is also a finite resource and has been valued for its rarity for thousands of years.

Another important characteristic of Bitcoin as a store of value is its durability. Unlike physical assets, Bitcoin is not subject to physical degradation or destruction, and it can be stored and transferred digitally with ease. This makes it a potentially more reliable store of value than other assets, which may deteriorate over time or be subject to damage or theft.

Bitcoin's relatively stable value over time also makes it a potentially valuable store of value. While the price of Bitcoin has been volatile in the past, its overall trend has been upward, and many investors see it as a potentially valuable long-term investment. As more people begin to recognize the potential value of Bitcoin as a store of value, demand for the cryptocurrency may increase, leading to further price appreciation.

There are, however, some potential risks and challenges associated with using Bitcoin as a store of value. One of the key risks is volatility. While Bitcoin's price has generally trended upward over the long term, it has been subject to significant short-term fluctuations, which can make it a risky investment for some investors. Additionally, the lack of regulation and oversight in the Bitcoin market can make it difficult for investors to assess the risks associated with investing in the cryptocurrency.

Despite these challenges, the potential for Bitcoin to be used as a store of value remains a key area of interest for investors and financial institutions. As the cryptocurrency market continues to evolve and mature, it is likely that we will see further developments in this area, and it is possible that Bitcoin may become an increasingly important part of the global financial system as a store of value.

The role of decentralized finance (DeFi) in the future of Bitcoin and financial transactions

Decentralized finance (DeFi) is an emerging field that seeks to create a more open, transparent, and accessible financial system using blockchain technology. DeFi platforms operate on decentralized networks, such as Ethereum, and allow users to access a wide range of financial services without relying on traditional banks or financial institutions. In recent years, DeFi has gained significant traction, with the total value locked in DeFi platforms reaching over $90 billion in August 2021.

The emergence of DeFi has significant implications for the future of Bitcoin and financial transactions. Bitcoin, as a decentralized digital currency, has already disrupted the traditional financial system by providing an alternative means of value transfer that is not controlled by any central authority. However, Bitcoin's functionality has so far been limited to basic transactions, such as peer-to-peer payments and currency exchange. DeFi, on the other hand, provides a platform for more complex financial transactions, such as lending and borrowing, derivatives trading, and insurance.

One of the main benefits of DeFi for Bitcoin is the potential to create a more efficient and accessible financial system. Decentralized platforms can reduce transaction costs and eliminate the need for intermediaries, making financial services more affordable and accessible to a wider range of people. Additionally, DeFi platforms can operate 24/7, providing users with round-the-clock access to financial services, which is not possible with traditional banks.

Another potential benefit of DeFi for Bitcoin is the potential for increased privacy and security. Decentralized networks can provide a high level of security, as they are not controlled by a single entity and are therefore less susceptible to attacks or data breaches. Additionally, some DeFi platforms use privacy-enhancing technologies, such as zero-knowledge proofs, to ensure that user data is kept private and confidential.

The role of DeFi in the future of Bitcoin is not limited to financial transactions. Decentralized networks can also provide a platform for new types of financial instruments, such as digital securities and tokenized assets. These instruments can be used to represent real-world assets, such as stocks, commodities, and real estate, and can be traded on decentralized exchanges. This has the potential to open up new investment opportunities for individuals and institutions and to create a more liquid and efficient market for asset trading.

However, there are also challenges and risks associated with DeFi. Decentralized networks can be susceptible to hacking and security breaches, and there is a risk of losing funds if users do not take adequate precautions. Additionally, the regulatory landscape for DeFi is still evolving, and there is uncertainty around how DeFi platforms will be regulated in the future.

In summary, DeFi has the potential to revolutionize the financial system by providing a more efficient, accessible, and secure platform for financial transactions. The integration of Bitcoin into the DeFi ecosystem could significantly enhance its functionality and open up new opportunities for investment and innovation. However, there are also risks and challenges associated with DeFi, and it is important for users to take adequate precautions and for regulators to establish a clear regulatory framework to ensure the safety and stability of the system.

Chapter 2: Bitcoin and Privacy

The importance of privacy in digital transactions

As the use of digital transactions becomes more prevalent in our daily lives, the issue of privacy has become increasingly important. With traditional financial systems, transactions are typically conducted through third-party intermediaries, such as banks or credit card companies, who collect and store personal information about individuals. However, with the rise of digital currencies like Bitcoin, individuals now have the potential to conduct financial transactions in a way that is more private and secure.

The importance of privacy in digital transactions can be traced back to the core values of personal freedom and individual autonomy. In an increasingly digital world, where personal information is being collected and stored by corporations and governments, the ability to conduct financial transactions without fear of intrusion or surveillance is becoming more important than ever.

In the context of Bitcoin, privacy is particularly important due to the decentralized nature of the system. Unlike traditional financial systems, where transactions are conducted through a centralized intermediary, Bitcoin transactions are processed and verified by a decentralized network of computers. This means that there is no central authority that can access or control users' personal information or financial data.

However, while Bitcoin transactions are generally considered to be more private than traditional financial transactions, there are still concerns about the level of privacy that the system provides. For example, while Bitcoin transactions are recorded on a public ledger, the identity of the individuals involved in the transaction is not disclosed. However, it is possible for individuals to link their Bitcoin addresses to their real-world identities through various means, such as social media profiles or online activity.

There are also concerns about the potential for Bitcoin transactions to be traced and monitored by law enforcement agencies or other organizations. While Bitcoin provides a level of privacy and anonymity that is not available with traditional financial systems, it is still possible for transactions to be traced back to their source through various means, such as IP addresses or transaction patterns.

Despite these concerns, the importance of privacy in digital transactions remains a key issue for many individuals and organizations. As the use of digital currencies like Bitcoin continues to grow, it is likely that we will see continued discussion and debate around the issue of privacy, and the potential for Bitcoin and other digital currencies to provide a more private and secure alternative to traditional financial systems.

The potential for Bitcoin to enhance privacy in financial transactions

Bitcoin is often touted as a privacy-focused cryptocurrency due to its pseudonymous nature. While Bitcoin transactions are publicly recorded on the blockchain, the identity of the parties involved in the transaction is not disclosed. However, there are still some privacy concerns related to Bitcoin transactions. In this chapter, we will explore the potential for Bitcoin to enhance privacy in financial transactions.

Firstly, it is important to note that Bitcoin is not completely private. While the identity of the parties involved in the transaction is not disclosed, the public nature of the blockchain means that transactions can be traced and analyzed. With the right tools and techniques, it is possible to trace the flow of funds through the blockchain and potentially identify the parties involved in a transaction.

To address these concerns, developers have been working on ways to enhance privacy on the Bitcoin network. One such technique is called coin mixing, also known as coin tumbling or coin shuffling. Coin mixing involves combining multiple Bitcoin transactions into a single transaction, making it difficult to trace the flow of funds.

Another technique that is being developed is called CoinJoin. This technique involves multiple parties joining together to form a single transaction. By doing this, it becomes difficult to determine which party sent which amount, enhancing privacy.

There are also various privacy-focused wallets available for Bitcoin users, such as the Wasabi wallet and the Samourai wallet. These wallets implement various techniques to enhance the privacy of Bitcoin transactions, such as coin mixing and the use of Tor to obfuscate IP addresses.

In addition to these techniques, there are also proposals to enhance privacy on the Bitcoin network through the use of new technologies, such as zero-knowledge proofs and bulletproofs. These technologies allow for the verification of transactions without disclosing the underlying data, thus enhancing privacy.

Overall, while Bitcoin is not completely private, there are various techniques and technologies being developed to enhance privacy on the network. It is important to continue to explore and develop these privacy-focused solutions to ensure that Bitcoin can be used as a truly private and secure form of digital currency.

The challenges and limitations of privacy in the Bitcoin system

The Bitcoin system is often touted as a secure and private means of conducting financial transactions. However, there are several challenges and limitations to privacy in the Bitcoin system that users and developers must consider.

One of the primary challenges to privacy in the Bitcoin system is the public ledger, known as the blockchain. While the blockchain ensures the integrity and immutability of transactions, it also allows anyone to view the transaction history of a particular Bitcoin address. This means that transactions on the Bitcoin network are not truly anonymous, but rather pseudonymous.

In addition, there are various ways in which Bitcoin transactions can be linked together, potentially revealing the identity of a user. For example, if a user consistently sends and receives Bitcoin from a particular address, this could reveal information about their financial activities and potentially their identity.

Another challenge to privacy in the Bitcoin system is the use of third-party services, such as Bitcoin exchanges and wallets. These services often require users to provide personal information, such as their name and address, which can be linked to their Bitcoin transactions.

Furthermore, there are limitations to the privacy-enhancing features of Bitcoin, such as the use of mixers or tumblers to obfuscate transaction trails. These services are not foolproof and can be vulnerable to attacks that compromise user privacy.

Developers are continually working on improving privacy features in the Bitcoin system, such as through the use of advanced cryptographic techniques like zero-knowledge proofs and ring signatures. However, these techniques are still in development and may have limitations or vulnerabilities that need to be addressed.

Overall, while the Bitcoin system offers some level of privacy and anonymity, there are still challenges and limitations that users and developers must consider. It is important for individuals to take steps to protect their privacy when using Bitcoin, such as using multiple addresses and avoiding linking transactions together. Additionally, continued research and development in privacy-enhancing technologies are essential to improve the privacy and security of the Bitcoin network.

Chapter 3: Bitcoin and Globalization
The potential impact of Bitcoin on international trade and commerce

Bitcoin, the first decentralized digital currency, has the potential to revolutionize the global financial system and reshape international trade and commerce. With its decentralized nature and lack of physical boundaries, Bitcoin has already shown potential as a means of cross-border transactions, enabling individuals and businesses to transfer funds instantaneously and inexpensively across borders.

The potential impact of Bitcoin on international trade and commerce is vast. Bitcoin has the potential to eliminate the need for intermediaries such as banks, credit card companies, and payment processors, reducing transaction costs and enabling direct peer-to-peer transactions. This could enable small businesses and individuals in developing countries to engage in cross-border trade and commerce without the need for traditional financial intermediaries.

Furthermore, the use of Bitcoin could help to facilitate trade in countries with less stable currencies or limited access to traditional banking services. Bitcoin transactions are borderless and require no third-party intermediaries, making it an attractive option for individuals and businesses looking to engage in international trade.

Bitcoin can also be used to bypass economic sanctions and restrictions, providing individuals and businesses with a means to engage in international trade even when traditional banking services are restricted. This can be particularly useful for individuals and businesses operating in countries subject to economic sanctions.

Another potential impact of Bitcoin on international trade and commerce is its potential to reduce the cost and time required for cross-border remittances. Currently, traditional remittance methods involve significant fees and can take days to complete. Bitcoin transactions, on the other hand, can be completed within minutes and involve only minimal transaction fees, making it an attractive option for individuals looking to send funds across borders quickly and inexpensively.

Despite its potential benefits, however, Bitcoin's impact on international trade and commerce is not without challenges. Bitcoin's volatile value, for example, can make it difficult for individuals and businesses to price goods and services in Bitcoin. Furthermore, Bitcoin's lack of widespread adoption and acceptance can limit its potential as a means of cross-border trade and commerce.

In conclusion, the potential impact of Bitcoin on international trade and commerce is vast, with the potential to reduce transaction costs, facilitate trade in countries with less stable currencies, and provide a means to bypass economic sanctions and restrictions. However, Bitcoin's impact is not without challenges, and continued development and adoption will be necessary to fully realize its potential as a means of cross-border trade and commerce.

The role of Bitcoin in enabling cross-border transactions

The emergence of Bitcoin has paved the way for a decentralized and borderless financial system that allows for transactions to occur seamlessly across countries and continents. Bitcoin's potential in enabling cross-border transactions has been recognized by many, including businesses and individuals looking for a more efficient and cost-effective way to transfer money internationally.

One of the major benefits of Bitcoin is that it eliminates the need for intermediaries such as banks and payment processors, which often charge high fees for cross-border transactions. By using Bitcoin, individuals and businesses can send and receive funds directly, without the need for costly middlemen. This not only reduces transaction costs but also allows for faster and more efficient transactions, as Bitcoin transactions can be processed within minutes.

Moreover, Bitcoin's decentralized nature means that it is not subject to the same regulations and restrictions as traditional financial institutions. This makes it an attractive option for individuals and businesses looking to circumvent government restrictions or avoid sanctions.

The role of Bitcoin in enabling cross-border transactions is particularly important for individuals in developing countries who may not have access to traditional financial services. With Bitcoin, anyone with an internet connection can participate in the global financial system and engage in cross-border transactions.

However, there are still some challenges and limitations associated with using Bitcoin for cross-border transactions. One of the biggest challenges is the volatility of the Bitcoin market, which can lead to fluctuations in the value of Bitcoin and make it difficult to predict the cost of cross-border transactions. Additionally, Bitcoin's relative lack of adoption and acceptance in some countries can make it difficult to find local businesses that accept Bitcoin as a form of payment.

Despite these challenges, the potential benefits of Bitcoin in enabling cross-border transactions are significant. As more individuals and businesses recognize the advantages of using Bitcoin for cross-border transactions, we can expect to see increased adoption and integration of Bitcoin into the global financial system. This could have far-reaching implications for international trade and commerce, as well as for the way we think about financial transactions across borders.

The potential for Bitcoin to reduce transaction costs and improve financial inclusion

Bitcoin's potential to reduce transaction costs and improve financial inclusion has been a significant driver of interest and investment in the cryptocurrency. The current global financial system is fraught with inefficiencies, particularly in cross-border transactions, that result in high costs and long wait times for users. Bitcoin, with its decentralized structure, has the potential to alleviate these issues and provide more efficient and cost-effective solutions.

One of the main ways in which Bitcoin can reduce transaction costs is by eliminating intermediaries such as banks and payment processors. These intermediaries often charge high fees for their services, which can be particularly burdensome for individuals and small businesses. Bitcoin transactions, on the other hand, typically involve low transaction fees that are paid to miners who maintain the network. This results in lower costs for users and could potentially lead to greater financial inclusion for individuals who may have previously been excluded from the traditional financial system due to high fees.

Another way in which Bitcoin can improve financial inclusion is by providing access to financial services to individuals who may not have had access to them before. Traditional financial institutions often require extensive documentation and credit histories, which can be a barrier to entry for individuals who do not have these credentials. Bitcoin, with its decentralized structure and lack of central authority, can provide access to financial services to anyone with an internet connection.

Bitcoin can also be particularly useful in enabling remittances, which are an important source of income for many families in developing countries. The current remittance market is dominated by intermediaries such as Western Union, which charge high fees for their services. Bitcoin, with its low transaction fees and fast transaction times, can provide a more cost-effective solution for individuals sending money across borders.

However, it is important to note that Bitcoin's potential to reduce transaction costs and improve financial inclusion is not without its limitations and challenges. One of the main challenges is the scalability of the Bitcoin network, which can result in slow transaction times and high fees during periods of high demand. Additionally, Bitcoin's volatility can make it difficult to use as a store of value, particularly for individuals in developing countries who may not have access to stable currencies.

Overall, while there are limitations and challenges to Bitcoin's potential to reduce transaction costs and improve financial inclusion, its decentralized structure and low transaction fees make it an attractive option for individuals and businesses seeking more efficient and cost-effective financial solutions.

Chapter 4: Bitcoin and Society

The potential social implications of Bitcoin

Bitcoin is not just a technological innovation; it is also a social phenomenon that is transforming the way we think about money and value. As a decentralized, peer-to-peer currency that operates outside the traditional banking system, Bitcoin has the potential to disrupt many aspects of our social and economic systems. In this section, we will explore some of the potential social implications of Bitcoin.

1. The Rise of a New Economic Elite

One of the key features of Bitcoin is its decentralization. Unlike traditional financial systems, which are controlled by a small group of institutions and individuals, Bitcoin is open to anyone who wants to participate. This means that anyone can mine, buy, or sell Bitcoins, regardless of their social or economic status.

While this democratization of finance is certainly a positive development, it also has the potential to create a new economic elite. As Bitcoin continues to grow in popularity and value, early adopters and investors stand to reap significant profits. This could lead to a situation where a small group of individuals hold a disproportionate amount of the world's wealth, based purely on their early adoption of Bitcoin.

2. New Forms of Economic Organization

Bitcoin is not just a currency; it is also a platform for innovation. One of the most exciting aspects of Bitcoin is the potential for new forms of economic organization that are not based on traditional hierarchies or structures.

For example, Bitcoin makes it possible to create decentralized autonomous organizations (DAOs), which are organizations that are run entirely on blockchain technology. These organizations are governed by smart contracts, which are self-executing contracts that enforce the rules and regulations of the organization. DAOs could potentially transform the way we think about business and governance, by providing a more transparent and democratic alternative to traditional organizations.

3. The Potential for Financial Inclusion

One of the biggest challenges facing the global economy is the problem of financial inclusion. Millions of people around the world do not have access to basic financial services, such as bank accounts or credit. This makes it difficult for them to participate in the global economy and to build wealth.

Bitcoin has the potential to change this. Because Bitcoin is decentralized and operates outside the traditional banking system, it is possible for anyone with an internet connection to participate in the Bitcoin economy. This could be particularly transformative for people in developing countries, who often lack access to traditional financial services.

4. Disrupting Traditional Power Structures

Bitcoin has the potential to disrupt many of the traditional power structures that underpin our social and economic systems. For example, Bitcoin could challenge the dominance of central banks, which currently control the supply of money and set monetary policy. By providing an alternative to traditional currencies, Bitcoin could empower individuals and communities to take control of their own financial destinies.

Similarly, Bitcoin could also challenge the dominance of large financial institutions, which currently control the vast majority of the world's wealth. By creating a decentralized, peer-to-peer financial system, Bitcoin could provide an alternative to traditional banking and investment models.

5. Privacy and Anonymity

Finally, Bitcoin has the potential to transform the way we think about privacy and anonymity. Because Bitcoin transactions are recorded on a public blockchain, they are theoretically traceable back to their origin. However, there are also ways to protect one's privacy and anonymity when using Bitcoin, such as through the use of mixing services or the creation of anonymous wallets.

This has important implications for individuals and communities who are concerned about their privacy and security, particularly in the wake of revelations about government surveillance and data breaches. Bitcoin provides a new way to protect one's financial privacy and security, and could potentially empower individuals and communities to take control of their own data.

In conclusion, Bitcoin has the potential to transform many aspects of our social and economic systems. While there are certainly challenges and risks associated with this new technology, there are also many opportunities for Bitcoin to drive positive change in society. Its potential to increase financial inclusion, enable faster and cheaper cross-border transactions, enhance privacy, and provide a decentralized alternative to traditional financial systems all offer exciting possibilities for the future. Additionally, Bitcoin's ability to function without intermediaries or central authorities has the potential to disrupt existing power structures, which could have significant implications for social and political systems. However, it is important to recognize that the adoption and evolution of Bitcoin is a complex process that involves a variety of stakeholders and interests, and its impact on society will depend on how it is developed and utilized in the coming years.

One of the potential social implications of Bitcoin is its ability to empower individuals and communities by providing them with greater financial autonomy. With Bitcoin, individuals have the ability to control their own funds without relying on traditional financial institutions or intermediaries. This can be particularly beneficial for people who are underserved by the current financial system, such as those who lack access to banking services or those who live in areas with high levels of economic instability. By providing a decentralized and open financial system, Bitcoin has the potential to increase financial inclusion and reduce economic inequality. However, it is important to note that Bitcoin is not a panacea for these issues, and there are still significant challenges that must be addressed to fully realize its potential to drive positive social change.

Another potential social implication of Bitcoin is its impact on the environment. The energy-intensive process of Bitcoin mining has raised concerns about its carbon footprint and contribution to climate change. While some argue that Bitcoin mining is driving the development of renewable energy sources, others believe that the environmental impact of Bitcoin is a significant concern that must be addressed. As the use of Bitcoin continues to grow, it will be important to consider its environmental impact and explore ways to mitigate its carbon footprint.

Overall, the potential social implications of Bitcoin are vast and complex. As this technology continues to evolve and become more integrated into our social and economic systems, it will be important to carefully consider its potential impact on society and work to maximize its positive effects while mitigating its risks and challenges.

The impact of Bitcoin on income inequality and wealth distribution

Bitcoin has the potential to have a significant impact on income inequality and wealth distribution. One of the key features of Bitcoin is its decentralized nature, which means that it is not controlled by any central authority or government. This feature is particularly attractive to those who are skeptical of traditional financial institutions and their role in perpetuating income inequality.

One potential impact of Bitcoin on income inequality is that it could provide access to financial services to individuals who are currently underserved or excluded from traditional banking systems. For example, people who live in rural or remote areas may find it difficult to access traditional banking services, which can make it difficult for them to save, invest, or participate in the global economy. With Bitcoin, however, all that is needed is an internet connection, which means that people anywhere in the world can access financial services.

Another way in which Bitcoin could impact income inequality is by providing an alternative store of value. Many people who live in countries with unstable currencies or high inflation rates turn to gold or other precious metals as a store of value. However, these metals can be difficult to store and transport, and they are not easily divisible. Bitcoin, on the other hand, is highly divisible and can be stored securely on a mobile device or computer. This could make it an attractive alternative for people who are looking for a store of value that is more accessible and convenient than traditional precious metals.

Despite these potential benefits, there are also concerns that Bitcoin could exacerbate income inequality. One concern is that early adopters of Bitcoin may accumulate a disproportionate amount of wealth, as has been the case with many other new technologies. This could create a new class of wealthy individuals who are able to accumulate even more wealth simply by holding onto their Bitcoin.

Another concern is that Bitcoin could be used to facilitate illegal activities, such as money laundering or tax evasion, which could further exacerbate income inequality. While it is true that Bitcoin transactions are anonymous, they are also recorded on a public ledger, which means that they can be traced back to their source. This could make it more difficult for criminals to use Bitcoin for illegal activities.

Overall, the impact of Bitcoin on income inequality and wealth distribution is still uncertain. While there are certainly risks and challenges associated with this new technology, there are also many opportunities for it to have a positive impact on the lives of people around the world. As with any new technology, it will be important to carefully consider the potential benefits and risks of Bitcoin, and to work to mitigate any negative impacts that it may have.

The role of Bitcoin in enabling new forms of economic organization and social change

Bitcoin has the potential to enable new forms of economic organization and social change due to its decentralized nature and ability to provide financial access to marginalized populations. This section will explore how Bitcoin can enable new economic models and social structures.

One of the most promising applications of Bitcoin is in enabling decentralized autonomous organizations (DAOs). A DAO is a decentralized organization that operates on the blockchain and is governed by smart contracts. It allows members to make decisions based on a democratic consensus mechanism rather than relying on a centralized authority. This creates an opportunity for new forms of economic organization that are more democratic and transparent.

Bitcoin also has the potential to promote social change by enabling financial access to marginalized populations. Many people around the world lack access to basic financial services such as bank accounts, credit cards, and loans. This is especially true in developing countries where a significant portion of the population is unbanked or underbanked. Bitcoin can enable financial access to these individuals by providing them with a means of storing and transferring value without the need for a traditional bank account.

Moreover, Bitcoin can also enable social change by facilitating the growth of decentralized marketplaces. Decentralized marketplaces are platforms that connect buyers and sellers directly, without the need for intermediaries. These marketplaces can provide individuals with greater economic autonomy and can help to break down monopolies and oligopolies that are often present in traditional markets.

Bitcoin can also facilitate social change by providing a means of supporting social causes and activism. Bitcoin donations can be made anonymously and directly to organizations without the need for intermediaries or government oversight. This provides individuals with a means of supporting causes that may be unpopular or controversial.

Overall, Bitcoin has the potential to enable new forms of economic organization and social change by providing financial access to marginalized populations, facilitating the growth of decentralized marketplaces, and supporting social causes and activism. However, it is important to recognize that these changes will not happen overnight and that there are still many challenges to be addressed, including the scalability of the Bitcoin network and the potential for centralization of mining power.

Chapter 5: Bitcoin and Regulation

The current regulatory landscape for Bitcoin and digital currencies

Bitcoin is a decentralized digital currency that operates outside the traditional banking system. It has attracted significant attention from regulators worldwide due to its potential to disrupt the existing financial system. As Bitcoin and other digital currencies become more popular, governments are grappling with how to regulate them. This chapter will provide an overview of the current regulatory landscape for Bitcoin and digital currencies and explore the various approaches taken by governments around the world.

Overview of the Current Regulatory Landscape:

The regulatory landscape for Bitcoin and other digital currencies varies significantly from country to country. Some countries have embraced Bitcoin and other digital currencies, while others have taken a more cautious approach. The following is an overview of the current regulatory landscape in some of the world's largest economies.

United States:

The United States has taken a relatively cautious approach to regulating Bitcoin and other digital currencies. In 2013, the Financial Crimes Enforcement Network

(FinCEN) issued guidance stating that digital currencies were subject to the same anti-money laundering (AML) and know-your-customer (KYC) regulations as traditional financial institutions. In 2015, the New York State Department of Financial Services (NYDFS) introduced the BitLicense, a regulatory framework for digital currency businesses operating in New York. The BitLicense has been criticized for being overly burdensome and has been blamed for driving many digital currency businesses out of the state.

Europe:

The regulatory landscape for Bitcoin and digital currencies in Europe varies significantly from country to country. In 2016, the European Union (EU) issued the Fifth Anti-Money Laundering Directive (5AMLD), which required digital currency exchanges to register with their national regulators and comply with AML and KYC regulations. Some countries, such as Germany and France, have taken a relatively supportive approach to digital currencies, while others, such as Russia, have taken a more cautious approach.

Asia:

The regulatory landscape for Bitcoin and digital currencies in Asia is also varied. In 2017, China banned initial coin offerings (ICOs) and closed down local digital currency exchanges. Japan, on the other hand, has taken a relatively supportive approach to digital currencies and has even recognized Bitcoin as a legal payment method.

Challenges Facing Bitcoin Regulation:

Regulating Bitcoin and other digital currencies presents several challenges. One of the biggest challenges is the global nature of digital currencies, which makes it difficult for regulators to control them. Digital currencies can be bought and sold from anywhere in the world, and many digital currency exchanges operate outside of traditional regulatory frameworks. Additionally, digital currencies are highly volatile, which makes it difficult for regulators to develop effective consumer protection measures.

Conclusion:

The regulatory landscape for Bitcoin and other digital currencies is complex and constantly evolving. Governments around the world are grappling with how to regulate digital currencies, and there is no consensus on how best to approach the issue. However, as digital currencies become more mainstream, it is likely that governments will continue to develop new regulatory frameworks to address the challenges posed by this new technology.

The challenges and opportunities of regulating Bitcoin

Bitcoin has gained increasing attention from regulators globally in recent years, leading to a patchwork of regulatory frameworks that are often fragmented and inconsistent. Regulating Bitcoin presents unique challenges and opportunities that need to be carefully considered.

One of the main challenges of regulating Bitcoin is its decentralized nature. Bitcoin operates on a peer-to-peer network that is not controlled by any central authority or institution. This makes it difficult for regulators to apply traditional regulatory frameworks that rely on centralized institutions such as banks or payment processors. As a result, regulators are often left grappling with how to monitor and enforce compliance on a decentralized network.

Another challenge of regulating Bitcoin is the lack of clarity around its legal status. In many jurisdictions, Bitcoin falls into a regulatory grey area, leaving businesses uncertain about their legal obligations and consumers unsure about their rights. This lack of clarity has led to an uneven regulatory landscape where some countries have embraced Bitcoin while others have outright banned it.

Despite the challenges, there are also opportunities for regulators to create a regulatory framework that supports the growth of Bitcoin while protecting consumers and promoting innovation. For example, regulators can work with industry players to establish industry standards and best practices. This can help to promote transparency and accountability in the industry, which can ultimately benefit consumers and the wider economy.

Regulators can also work with Bitcoin businesses to promote financial inclusion. One of the main advantages of Bitcoin is its ability to enable low-cost, cross-border transactions, making it an attractive option for those who are underbanked or excluded from the traditional financial system. Regulators can support the growth of Bitcoin by creating policies that encourage financial inclusion and by working with Bitcoin businesses to ensure that they are providing services that are accessible to all.

Finally, regulators can play a critical role in protecting consumers from fraud and other illicit activities. Bitcoin has been associated with a number of high-profile scams and hacks, which can erode public trust in the technology. Regulators can help to protect consumers by creating policies that require Bitcoin businesses to implement strong security measures and by enforcing penalties against those who engage in fraudulent or illegal activities.

In summary, regulating Bitcoin presents both challenges and opportunities. While its decentralized nature poses unique challenges for regulators, there are also opportunities to promote innovation, financial inclusion, and consumer protection. As the regulatory landscape continues to evolve, it will be important for regulators to strike a balance between promoting innovation and protecting consumers.

The potential for government intervention in the Bitcoin system

Bitcoin is a decentralized system that operates independently of any government or central authority. As a result, it has been a challenge for regulators to determine how best to approach Bitcoin and other digital currencies. While some governments have embraced Bitcoin, others have been more skeptical, viewing it as a threat to their traditional financial systems.

One of the main concerns that governments have with Bitcoin is its potential use for illegal activities, such as money laundering and terrorist financing. This has led to calls for increased regulation of the Bitcoin system. However, there are challenges associated with regulating a decentralized system like Bitcoin. For example, it is difficult to identify and monitor individual users on the Bitcoin network, making it challenging to enforce regulations.

Despite these challenges, there is also an opportunity for governments to embrace Bitcoin and work with the industry to create a regulatory framework that supports innovation while protecting consumers and preventing illegal activities. This could involve measures such as requiring Bitcoin businesses to comply with Know Your Customer (KYC) and Anti-Money Laundering (AML) regulations, as well as implementing taxes on Bitcoin transactions.

One potential area for government intervention in the Bitcoin system is the regulation of exchanges and other Bitcoin businesses. Exchanges are often the point of entry and exit for Bitcoin users, and they can be a key target for regulators seeking to prevent illegal activities. Governments could require exchanges to be licensed and regulated, similar to traditional financial institutions, and impose strict reporting requirements to ensure that they are complying with regulations.

Another area where government intervention may be necessary is in the area of taxation. While Bitcoin is often touted as a tax-free currency, governments are increasingly taking steps to ensure that Bitcoin transactions are subject to the same tax laws as traditional financial transactions. This could involve imposing taxes on Bitcoin transactions, or requiring Bitcoin users to report their transactions to tax authorities.

Ultimately, the potential for government intervention in the Bitcoin system is a complex issue that will require careful consideration and collaboration between industry stakeholders and regulators. While it is important to protect consumers and prevent illegal activities, it is also important to avoid stifling innovation and growth in the Bitcoin industry. As the regulatory landscape continues to evolve, it will be important for governments to strike a balance between these competing priorities.

Conclusion

The broader implications of Bitcoin beyond finance, including privacy, globalization, and societal impact

Bitcoin is a digital currency that has gained significant attention since its creation in 2009. While initially viewed as a niche technology, Bitcoin has increasingly gained mainstream acceptance and adoption in recent years. In addition to its potential impact on the financial system, Bitcoin also has broader implications for areas such as privacy, globalization, and society as a whole. This section will explore these broader implications of Bitcoin and its potential impact beyond finance.

One of the key areas where Bitcoin has the potential to make a significant impact is in the area of privacy. The decentralized nature of the Bitcoin network means that users can transact without the need for intermediaries such as banks. This can provide greater privacy and anonymity for users, particularly those in countries where financial privacy is limited. However, as discussed in Chapter 2, there are also challenges and limitations to privacy in the Bitcoin system, particularly in light of the increasing sophistication of blockchain analysis techniques.

Another area where Bitcoin has the potential to make a significant impact is in the area of globalization. The ability to transact with anyone, anywhere in the world, without the need for intermediaries, can greatly facilitate international trade and commerce. This can provide benefits to both individuals and businesses, particularly those in developing countries where access to traditional financial services may be limited. As discussed in Chapter 3, Bitcoin also has the potential to reduce transaction costs and improve financial inclusion, which can have a significant impact on global economic growth.

Beyond finance, Bitcoin also has the potential to enable new forms of economic organization and social change. The ability to transact without intermediaries and the potential for decentralized decision-making can provide new opportunities for individuals and communities to collaborate and organize in ways that were previously impossible. As discussed in Chapter 4, Bitcoin can also have an impact on income inequality and wealth distribution, potentially enabling greater economic empowerment for marginalized communities.

However, the potential impact of Bitcoin beyond finance is not without its challenges. As discussed in Chapter 5, the regulatory landscape for Bitcoin is complex and evolving, with different countries taking different approaches to regulation. There is also the potential for government intervention in the Bitcoin system, particularly in the areas of taxation and law enforcement.

Overall, the potential impact of Bitcoin beyond finance is vast and multifaceted. While there are certainly challenges and risks associated with this new technology, there are also many opportunities for positive change and transformation. As Bitcoin and other cryptocurrencies continue to evolve, it will be important to carefully consider the broader implications of these technologies and to develop strategies for maximizing their potential benefits while mitigating their potential risks.

The potential for further development and innovation in the Bitcoin system

Bitcoin is a relatively new technology, and as such, it is likely to continue to evolve and develop over time. There are many potential areas for further innovation and development in the Bitcoin system, ranging from technical improvements to new use cases for the technology.

One potential area for further development in the Bitcoin system is the improvement of the user experience. While Bitcoin has made great strides in recent years to become more user-friendly, it is still somewhat challenging for the average person to use and understand. Improvements in user experience could include the development of more intuitive user interfaces and the simplification of the process for buying and selling Bitcoin.

Another potential area for further development in the Bitcoin system is the improvement of scalability. Currently, the Bitcoin network can only process a limited number of transactions per second, which limits its usefulness in certain applications. However, there are many proposed solutions to this problem, including the development of second-layer protocols like the Lightning Network and the implementation of new consensus mechanisms like Proof of Stake.

In addition to these technical improvements, there are also many potential new use cases for the Bitcoin system. For example, Bitcoin could be used as a means of creating decentralized social networks, where users control their own data and are not subject to the whims of centralized corporations. Bitcoin could also be used as a means of creating decentralized marketplaces, where users can buy and sell goods and services without the need for intermediaries.

Overall, the potential for further development and innovation in the Bitcoin system is vast. While there are certainly challenges and risks associated with this new technology, there are also many opportunities for those who are willing to invest in its future. As the world becomes increasingly digital, Bitcoin has the potential to play an increasingly important role in our economic and social systems.

The importance of continued research and discussion around the future of Bitcoin and its impact on society

Bitcoin has already made a significant impact on the world of finance and technology, and its potential for further growth and development is still being explored. As the technology evolves and new use cases emerge, it is important to continue researching and discussing the future of Bitcoin and its impact on society.

One key area for continued research and discussion is the impact of Bitcoin on economic and social inequality. While Bitcoin has the potential to democratize financial systems and increase access to capital, it could also exacerbate existing wealth disparities. It is important to consider ways in which the technology can be leveraged to promote greater equality and inclusion.

Another area for continued research is the role of Bitcoin in promoting privacy and data security. As digital transactions become increasingly ubiquitous, the need for robust privacy protections becomes more urgent. Bitcoin's decentralized architecture and encryption protocols have the potential to provide greater security and anonymity than traditional financial systems, but it is important to study and address any vulnerabilities or risks associated with the technology.

Finally, it is important to consider the potential for further innovation and development within the Bitcoin system itself. As new use cases emerge and the technology continues to evolve, there may be opportunities for further innovation in areas such as scalability, usability, and interoperability. It is important to encourage ongoing research and development in these areas to ensure that Bitcoin can continue to meet the needs of users and stakeholders.

In conclusion, Bitcoin is a complex and rapidly evolving technology with broad implications for finance, privacy, globalization, and social organization. As the technology continues to develop, it is important to remain engaged in ongoing research and discussion to ensure that it can be leveraged for positive social and economic outcomes. Whether through increased financial inclusion, greater privacy protections, or new forms of social and economic organization, Bitcoin has the potential to be a powerful force for change in the years and decades to come.

THE END

Key Terms and Definitions

To help you better understand the language and concepts related to aging and older adults, below you will find a list of key terms and their definitions.

1. Bitcoin: A digital currency that operates on a decentralized blockchain network without the need for a central authority.

2. Blockchain: A decentralized digital ledger of transactions that is verified by a network of computers.

3. Cryptocurrency: A digital asset that is designed to work as a medium of exchange, using cryptography to secure transactions and control the creation of new units.

4. Decentralization: The distribution of power and decision-making across a network of nodes, rather than being controlled by a central authority.

5. Mining: The process by which new Bitcoins are created and transactions are verified on the blockchain network.

6. Wallet: A software program that stores private keys used to access and spend Bitcoin and other cryptocurrencies.

7. Fork: A split in the blockchain network that creates two separate versions of the blockchain, often due to disagreements within the community.

8. Smart contract: A self-executing contract that contains the terms of the agreement between parties and is automatically enforced by the blockchain network.

9. Public key cryptography: A cryptographic system that uses a pair of keys, a public key, and a private key, to encrypt and decrypt data and authenticate digital signatures.

10. Financial inclusion: The access to financial services and products that are affordable and suited to individual needs, especially among disadvantaged and marginalized communities.

Supporting Materials
Bitcoin Whitepaper

According to the original Bitcoin whitepaper (https://bitcoin.org/bitcoin.pdf) that was authored by Satoshi Nakamoto and titled "Bitcoin: A Peer-to-Peer Electronic Cash System.", here are the page numbers that could be covered in each book:

Book 1/3:

Introduction: Pages 1-2

Chapter 1: "Introduction" section on Page 1

Chapter 2: "Transactions" section on Pages 2-4

Chapter 3: "Timestamp Server" section on Pages 4-5

Chapter 4: "Proof-of-Work" section on Pages 5-7

Chapter 5: "Network" section on Pages 7-8

Conclusion: Pages 8-9

Book 2/3:

Introduction: Pages 1-2

Chapter 1: "Introduction" section on Page 1

Chapter 2: "The Economics of Bitcoin" section on Pages 2-3

Chapter 3: "Bitcoin and Financial Inclusion" section on Pages 3-4

Chapter 4: "Bitcoin and Social Implications" section on Pages 4-6

Chapter 5: "Bitcoin and Income Inequality" section on Pages 6-7

Conclusion: Pages 8-9

Book 3/3:

Introduction: Pages 1-2

Chapter 1: "Introduction" section on Page 1

Chapter 2: "Future Directions" section on Pages 2-3

Chapter 3: "Regulatory Landscape" section on Pages 3-4

Chapter 4: "Potential Applications" section on Pages 4-5

Chapter 5: "Bitcoin and the Environment" section on Pages 5-6

Conclusion: Pages 8-9

Potential References

Introduction

- Antonopoulos, A. M. (2014). Mastering Bitcoin: Unlocking Digital Cryptocurrencies. O'Reilly Media, Inc.
- Nakamoto, S. (2008). Bitcoin: A Peer-to-Peer Electronic Cash System. https://bitcoin.org/bitcoin.pdf

Chapter 1: Bitcoin and the Future of Finance

- Casey, M. J., & Vigna, P. (2018). The Truth Machine: The Blockchain and the Future of Everything. St. Martin's Press.
- Tapscott, D., & Tapscott, A. (2016). Blockchain revolution: how the technology behind bitcoin is changing money, business, and the world. Penguin.

Chapter 2: Bitcoin and Privacy

- Greenberg, A. (2014). Darkode Shutdown Proves the Internet Can Finally Fight Cybercrime. Wired. https://www.wired.com/2015/07/darkode-shutdown-proves-the-internet-can-finally-fight-cybercrime/
- Narayanan, A., Bonneau, J., Felten, E., Miller, A., & Goldfeder, S. (2016). Bitcoin and Cryptocurrency Technologies: A Comprehensive Introduction. Princeton University Press.

Chapter 3: Bitcoin and Globalization

- Antonopoulos, A. M. (2014). The Internet of Money. Merkle Bloom LLC.

- Fung, B., & Shiller, R. J. (2017). Can Bitcoin Be a Stable Currency? Brookings Papers on Economic Activity, 2017(2), 89-150.

Chapter 4: Bitcoin and Society

- Bjerg, O. (2016). How is Bitcoin money? Theory, Culture & Society, 33(1), 53-72.
- Mougayar, W. (2016). The Business Blockchain: Promise, Practice, and Application of the Next Internet Technology. John Wiley & Sons.

Chapter 5: Bitcoin and Regulation

- European Parliament. (2016). Virtual currencies and central banks monetary policy: challenges ahead. Directorate-General for Internal Policies, Policy Department A: Economic and Scientific Policy.
- FinCEN. (2013). Application of FinCEN's Regulations to Persons Administering, Exchanging, or Using Virtual Currencies. https://www.fincen.gov/sites/default/files/shared/FIN-2013-G001.pdf

Conclusion

- Buterin, V. (2014). A Next-Generation Smart Contract and Decentralized Application Platform. https://github.com/ethereum/wiki/wiki/White-Paper

- Swan, M. (2015). Blockchain: Blueprint for a New Economy. O'Reilly Media, Inc.

www.ingramcontent.com/pod-product-compliance
Lightning Source LLC
LaVergne TN
LVHW012127070526
838202LV00056B/5893